Note from the Author:

I hope that you all enjoy reading this book.

writing what I would like to call a spiritual slashed with a

enjoy and let me know what you think.

Queen

MW01047225

Acknowledgements

I would like to thank the Most High for all the wisdom that he has given me up to this point. To all my spirit guides who walk with me and protect me, I honor you all. No disrespect is given to any of you.

Thank you Papa Joe for all your wisdom and guidance!

ANGEL'S ONYX

CHAPTER 1

Sweetness stepped out of the shower around seven o'clock that night feeling like she was on top of the world. It was her twenty first birthday, and she had made some serious plans to hang out with her girls tonight. Her clothes had been laid out perfectly across her bed, as if they were waiting on her voluptuous body to fill them up.

Sweetness had come into her womanhood at an early age of eight. Her mother had tried to keep her inside the house under lock and key, but that didn't stop her from blossoming out all over. Her mother had told her that the reason she had matured so quickly was because of her Ancestors Puerto Rican blood coursing thru her African veins. But by no means did she consider herself a half-breed. In her eyes she was an all black from head to toe.

Sweetness had been a wanderer by nature. She often found herself becoming bored very easily. She loved change. At times it didn't matter if it was good or bad as long as the change kept her interest up. There were times where everything had to be her way, or no way. There was no compromising with her or with her passion when it tended to rise up in her veins causing her blood to boil. At those times, everyone stayed cleared of her, for she was liken unto a she-demon. Literally!

Sweetness dried herself off slowly enjoying the smooth texture of her towel all over her body. In her mind she was a Queen, and real Queens deserved good things. She walked over to her bed and began dressing herself. After dressing herself, she walked over to her full-length mirror and stared at herself. Damn did she look good! She had chosen to wear an army fatigue tank top, cut off at the waist to reveal her butterfly belly button, and butterfly tattoo on her lower back. Sweetness also was wearing a brown mini skirt showing off the fullness of her shapely legs. She had ordered these pair of knee length camouflage timberland boots from on-line to go with her shirt. She had just started locking her hair to form dreads, so she placed a brown kangol brim on top of her head. Her make up was banging and her silver hoop earrings that her little sister Chance had given her for her birthday made her look really hot. As she stood there admiring herself her cell phone began ringing. She walked over to her bed and picked it up to answer it.

"Hello", she said answering the phone.

"What's up baby!" she heard her man Onyx say to her.

"Nothing, just getting ready to go out with my girls and shit," Sweetness answered.

"That's cool," Onyx replied." I want to see you before you go out."

"C'mon on man, I don't feel like playing with you tonight."

"Why you always thinking that all I want to do is fuck you all the time?"

"Because ever since you found that I can't have children, and nor do I have a period anymore you always want to keep me laying on my backside, and shit," she said to him.

"Look baby, I got a surprise for you," he said to her desperately.

Sweetness began smiling really hard when she heard that. She knew that his surprises were always big surprises.

"What kind of a surprise?" she asked smiling.

He began smiling as well.

"If you meet me right now on the corner of Rock Quarry and Crosslink at Burger King, I'll take you to your surprise."

"Okay Onyx. I'll be there in ten minutes."

Sweetness closed her phone before Onyx could tell her bye. She grabbed the keys to her Explorer and went down stairs. She saw her mother and Chance sitting on the sofa in the living room watching television.

"Okay ya'll I I'll be back after while," she spoke to them.

Her mother looked up at her oldest daughter.

"Angel Jones, be careful out there tonight," she said to her.

"Mommy I will be. It's my birthday. I'm going to enjoy myself tonight," she said happily.

"Angel I know that it's your birthday, and I want to you to have fun, but do it carefully. That moon is shining bright tonight, and anything can happen," her mother said back to her.

"Alright ma, there you go with that superstitious stuff again."

Sweetness leaned over the sofa and kissed her mother on the cheek. "What ever Angel," she said to her. "But in any case be careful."

Sweetness exited out the front door, got into her SUV and drove off.

Maria sat there and watched her daughter leave. Turning twenty-one was a big step in the Jones's women life. It not only meant that you were really now an adult, but to them so much more. For there was something more than blood which flowed thru their veins and she began to pray for her daughter.

CHAPTER 2

The little girl sat in a corner in the dark room that used to be someone's bedroom. she had been had snatched from off the street near her home that evening, and had taken to an abandon house on Bragg St. in southeast Raleigh. The man had been following orders from the Voice that often spoke within his mind telling him what to do with the young girls that he kidnapped and molested. Each girl had been born on the same day, February 2nd, and each one bore the symbol of an unusual birthmark on her right thigh. The birthmark resembled a huge purple grape with exception of hair growing from it. The Man did not know why the Voice always told him to go out and search for these types of young girls bearing that birthmark. It was as if the Voice was searching for something or someone. The little girl heard footsteps coming closer to her as she tried her best to scream, but no sound escaped from her lips. All she knew that this was not her home and she was scared of those heavy foot steps walking around the upstairs night after night.

Suddenly the door opened up and the Man slid a food tray to her.

"Eat little one, you must keep up your strength."

The little girl kicked the tray of food to the side.

"Please baby, eat," she heard him say as if in desperation.

"No," she cried. "I want to go home to my Mommy!"

"That's not possible," he said calmly.

"Why?" she asked tearfully.

"I need you," he answered her.

The little girl began crying violently. She was too young to understand what he meant, but she knew that he meant to harm her in a way that her Mother had warned her about.

"Please don't hurt me," she cried. "I'm only nine years old!"

"Yes I know." He slid the tray of food back to her. "Eat now and rest."

Slowly she reached over and pulled the tray of food to her. On the tray was a big red shiny apple with a banana and a pear.

She took the apple off the tray and stared into its redness.

"Aaaah!" she screamed as she dropped the apple and it hit the floor.

CHAPTER 3

Onyx was beginning to become impatient waiting for Sweetness to arrive at their meeting place. He loved her so much, but to him she needs to learn to be time conscious and arrive on time, especially since he had told her about her surprise. He sat in his black on black 2006 Denali looking at himself in the rearview mirror. His skin complexion was a deep dark chocolate without a single blemish. He had started using Proactive on his face when he saw an infomercial with Diddy advertising its use. After all he himself had to preserve his own sexiness as well.He wore his hair cut close with evenly shaped sideburns and a neatly trimmed goatee to match. Even though he was a hustler, he did not like sporting those fronts in his mouth, for his teeth were perfectly straight and pearly white. Onyx worked out every day for about an hour, so his torso was ridiculously muscular. Onyx was just plain gorgeous. Many women flung themselves at him, but he only had eyes for Sweetness.

Just as he was thinking about Sweetness, she had turned into Burger King and parked her Explorer right beside his Denali.Sweetness got out of her truck and hopped into the passenger side of his SUV.Onyx leaned over and kissed her on the lips.

"Damn you taste so sweet," he said licking his lips.

"That's why they call me Sweetness," she said teasingly.

"Alright now, slow your row," he said trying to act like he was jealous.

"Baby you know you the only one hitting this," Sweetness said taking his hands and placing them on her breasts.

"Now see you about to make this thing hard," he said glancing down at his penis.

"Okay I'm a chill, but you be knowing that as good as your dick is why would I fuck with anybody else?"

Onyx looked at her with a huge smile on his face. He loved it when Sweetness complimented him on his lovemaking. To him every time he entered her, it became more spiritual each time. It was like he was caught up a in a warm bath of frankincense and myrrh and he just could not get enough of her essence. To Onyx it was as if she took him to places; to other realms in the universe, where they were the only two beings in existence, like Adam and Eve were the in Garden of Eden. Before they got kicked out of the garden and they lived in paradise. Onyx could not explain it, but he always felt that Sweetness didn't belong in this world, and all he wanted to do was protect her and keep her safe. There had been times when she would tell him that she dreamed about something pertaining to him and it would come true that same day. Sweetness was special, and he vowed that he would always be with her, even unto death.

"Where's my surprise at?" Sweetness asked him, looking in the back seat of the Denali.

"Fasten your seat belt, we about to go for a ride."

She fasten her seat belt as he pulled out of the parking lot and turned right driving towards Walnut Creek Amphitheater.

CHAPTER 4

When Onyx and Sweetness came to the second stop light by Southeast Raleigh High School, he opened up the glove compartment, pulled out a white scarf and told her to tie it around her eyes so that she could not see anything. Sweetness did as she was told and once the scarf was tightly secured around her face covering her eyes, Onyx began driving again.

Sweetness had no idea where they were going or what he was up to, but she knew that it had to be something special. Once Onyx finally arrived at their destination, he pulled up to the side of the street and asked Sweetness to wait for him to get her out of the truck. He opened his door then walked around to the passenger side to let her out. Then taking her hand he guided her up the sidewalk and towards her surprise. He then took out a slide card like the ones they use at Hotels and used it to open the door. Once the door was opened, he guided her inside the place where her surprise was and closed the door behind them. Sweetness could smell her favorite incense burning, black sandalwood.

"Oh that smells so good," she said to him

"It's your favorite incense," he replied.

She reached up to take her blindfold off.

"Do not be in a rush," Onyx said to her, pushing her arms down.

"I can't wait to see where we are," she said to him. "This better not be a Hotel we are in."

"Baby its better than that," he said to her happily. "Stand right here."

Onyx then placed one of the cards he used to open the door in her right hand. Then he placed one single rose in her left hand. He then walked behind her and removed her blindfold. Sweetness blinked eyes her little to allow them to become adjusted to the lights. She then looked down at the items he had placed inside her hands. She knew that the rose meant that he loved her, but what was up with the key card?Sweetness then looked at her surroundings. She could tell that they both were standing in the middle of a foyer of a house.

"Where are we?" she asked him nervously.

"Baby this is your surprise!" he exclaimed.

"My- my surprise?" she stammered.

"Yes baby, take my hand and follow me."

Onyx took her hand and guided her into the living room. Sweetness could not believe her eyes. The room was decorated in African Art with African paintings covering the walls. The carpet was a soft lavender and very plush with a hint of platinum. Each wall was painted a different shade of lavender. The sofa was a white sectional formed in a semi circle in the middle of the room. There was a fireplace to the right of her, with a huge painting of the both of them hanging over it. She was dumb struck.

"What is this Onyx?" she asked him softly.

"Baby it's our new home," he exclaimed happily.

"Our what?"

"Sweetness it's our place baby," he said softly.

"It's ours?"

"Yes I bought this home for the both of us. You and I."

He took her by the hand and led her to the couch.

"That card which you are holding is your key to your home."

"I can't believe that you did this for me," she said excitedly. "This is so amazing!"

Onyx reached down under the sofa and brought out a tiny jewelry box. He opened it up, took out the ring, and got down on one knee.

"Angel Jones will you marry me so that we can fill this house up with love and maybe one day adopt two children?"

Tears began forming in Sweetness eyes.

"Hell yes!" she exclaimed, through her tears "Hell yes!"

Onyx picked her up off the sofa and carried her upstairs to the master bedroom. Sweetness could not believe her eyes when she saw how he had laid out the bedroom. Everything was white and lavender with a soft burgundy. Those were her favorite colors.

"I can't believe that you did all this for me," she whispered to him.

"Sweetness, I love your ass so much. You really do not know how much," he said to her.

Sweetness kissed him on his third eye. As her lips touched his forehead, she saw his image lying in an abandoned room. She pulled back from him suddenly with an ashen look on her face.

"What's wrong Sweetness?" Onyx asked her, puzzled by the look on her face.

Sweetness shook her head as if to shake the vision from her minds eye.

"Nothing baby," she lied.

"What you probably just thought about how young you are and me asking you to marry me at such a young age?"

"Yeah baby, that's it," she answered lying to him again.

"Well don't worry about that. I know that we have to wait a while before we get married. You still have to go to college and shit. I just want to make sure that you have all that you need with me."

Sweetness embraced him.

"I know you do Onyx," she said softly.

She reached up and kissed him again.

"Now give me some of that big juicy ass dick."

"What about your girls?"

"Man those heifers can wait. I need to you right now."

"Take off those clothes," he said to her, as she began undressing before he had told her to.

Sweetness looked at him with her big brown eyes, for she knew that she was about to get served righteously.

CHAPTER 5

Maria Jones looked at the clock when it struck midnight. It was time to prepare for Angel's homecoming. That's what her grandmother had called her journey when she had turned twenty-one.Maria got up from the sofa and went downstairs into the basement. She walked over towards the dryer and pushed a red button hanging on the wall. The wall behind the dryer slid to the side as she entered into her secret room. In the middle of the room was an altar standing 3 feet off the ground. On the altar were a ram's head, purple candle and a black mask. She placed the mask on her face and lit the purple candle. Slowly she bent down and kissed the Ram's head 3 times. She stepped back and lifted her arms high above her head.Maria began chanting.

"I summon the first mother, the second mother, and the third mother, the fourth mother, the fifth mother, the sixth mother, the seventh mother, the eighth mother, the ninth mother. As I call one, I call all."

Each one began appearing at her summons, surrounding her in a circle.

Each one resembled each other in their features.

"I call upon the Mother of us all, please come for it is time."

As she spoke a gust of wind appeared out of nowhere, and this beautiful woman steppedout of its midst. She was clothed in a multi- colored gown. On her right wrist she wore nine copper bracelets, and in her left hand she carried a long horsetail whip.

"Where is Angel," the woman asked Maria.

"She has gone out," Maria answered.

"Why did you let her go on this night, February 2nd?" the woman asked her.

"She has a mind of her own, maman. She is truly your daughter."

"Do you know what will happen when the clock strikes 3?"

"Yes, Maman."

"It is dangerous for her to be out. She will be like a ripe apple."

This I know maman, but her anger is fierce and I did not want to make her stay in on her born day."

The woman spun around the room and looked at her Ancient daughters.

"Her blood runs hotter in her veins than any of you. She has been chosen."

The nine Ancient daughters bowed their heads in reference to their Mother.

"I must go to her."

The woman vanished with the wind.

Maria fell to her knees in front of the Ancient daughters.

One of the Ancient daughters spoke. "We all have been waiting for this day. Let prophecy be fulfilled."

Once those words were spoken, the nine Ancient daughters vanished also. Maria rose up from the floor and removed the mask. All she could do now was wait for Angel to come back home.

CHAPTER 6

After Sweetness and Onyx had finished making love, she laid there in their bed feeling like she was on top of the world. Her man had bought her house for her birthday! He had even furnished and decorated it in all her favorite colors. Even the furnishings had been to her liking. Onyx hustled, so she hoped that she would not have to stay in the big four-bedroom house all by herself. For some reason being alone gave her the creeps.

It seemed like she was always sensing something waiting to grab her up when she was by herself. Sometimes at night she could feel a presence holding her down, trying to strangle her and it seemed as if she had no usage of her vocal chords to scream, nor movement of her limbs to move. During these times she would call upon Jesus and the energy would leave as sudden as it came.

Sweetness glanced over at the clock on the dresser and it read 1:45 am. She was just about to wake Onyx up when she heard his cell phone ringing.

"Baby wake up," she said slightly shaking him to wake up.

"I know Sweetness," he said waking up. "I hear it."

Onyx answered the phone and it was his homey Sal telling him to get to the block fast because something was going down with one of his houses. He hung the phone up.

All of sudden Sweetness saw that vision again.

"Please Onyx don't leave," she began pleading with him.

"Bay, I won't be long," he said to her, getting up out of the bed and reaching for his pants.

"Sweetie I wanted some more."

"When I get back home, you can have all of this sweet dick, but right now I have to handle this."

Sweetness jumped out of the bed. "I'm a go with you then."

"No baby stay here," he demanded. "I will be right back."

Onyx picked her up and laid her back on the bed, kissing her at the same time.

"I want to know how it's going to feel coming home to you and having your sweet ass waiting for me every night."

"Just like this," she said grinding her hips against his.

"Stop playing girl, "he said laughing. "I will break you off some more when I get back."

Sweetness released him from her embrace and fell back on the bed. The vision of him laying on the floor in an abandon house kept appearing in her mind.

"Please be safe baby," she said with wariness in her voice.

"Stop stressing," he replied. "Everything will be ok."

Onyx finished getting dressed and left.

When Onyx left the house, Sweetness decided that she would do some exploring of the rest of the house. She glanced at the clock and it said 3:00 am. All of sudden her head started hurting. She had been experiencing headaches before, but not like this. Her head was hurting so bad that she fell back on the bed with tears in her eyes.

"What the fuck is this?" she yelled out in pain.

It felt as if a football was being kicked around in her head. Then suddenly as it came it left. She started to get up to the bathroom to get a drink of water, when she felt this force push her back on the bed. Fear began to overtake her body causing her to panic.

Sweetness could feel the blood in her veins becoming hotter. Her whole body seemed as if it was on fire. Something had her pinned down against the bed and she could not move. The next thing she knew she was convulsing and shaking badly on top of the bed. Her body began levitating a few inches off the bed. She could not scream nor could she move. The force released her and she fell back onto the bed. As she stared up into the ceiling, she saw what appeared to be a black ankh forming in the middle of the ceiling. Then she began seeing faces of women looking down at her. She began to whimper in fright, for her voice had left her and she could not speak. Suddenly she heard this whisper of a voice telling her to move over for she was coming in.

Sweetness drifted off into unconscious.

CHAPTER 7

The Man heard the little girl's screams, and began chuckling to himself. This little girl that he was holding captive in the other room was the one that he believed that the Voice had been searching for. All the others had chosen another piece of fruit to eat and had not seen what this girl had seen. She was special indeed! The Voice had told him that he could do whatever he pleased with the others, for they were of no use to him. Neither one of them possessed the sight, nor had they been attracted to the red apple that this girl had chosen. The Man had a cruel appetite for young flesh in a sadistic kind of way. He knew that they could not fight back when he began raping them. All the girls had been at the age of nine, and some of their young bodies had not yet been developed. Their vaginas had been so tight and pure; that once he entered them he would inhale the aroma of their innocence causing his penis to become harder. He would never pump himself into the girls, but just enter them to get that rush of pure essence. He then would slice their throats and drink their blood. One cup of virgin's blood always seems to satisfy his thirst for their souls.

The little girl screams made him desire her, but he knew that she could not be touched. She was special for she had chosen the red apple, and seen the souls of the other girls that he had murdered. He could smell the essence of her being through the walls, and it made him feel as if his whole being was being embraced by a cool gentle breeze of purity. Thesensation of all that raw energy was making the thirst for her blood unbearable to withstand. At that moment he did not care what the Voice wanted, he was going to take her and quench his need for her blood.

As he began moving towards the door, all of a sudden a huge force blew him back against the wall. The Man was not small in his stature. The force was so strong that when he hit the wall, the whole room shook. He tried to move, but the force was holding him. He felt himself becoming weak, and could no longer struggle with what was holding him against the wall. Then he heard what sounded like a thousand wings fluttering in his ears, at first it was muffled, but as it got louder, he knew that the Voice was coming and there was nothing he could do to escape its wrath.

"What the fuck were you about to do?" he heard the Voice say to him.

"I was going to check on the girl," he answered in fright.

"You are lying," the Voice yelled.

"No- no," he stammered.

"How can you deceive the Father of Lies?" the Voice asked him.

"I wanted to surprise you, for we have the one that you have been searching for," he answered him.

"I already know," the Voice said to him. "But you wanted her for yourself."

"Her essence makes me desire her blood."

"You can not have this one for she belongs to me. She is the daughter of a very powerful Orisha whose voice is like the thunder and who carries fire in his veins. This girl is connected to another who is much older, and they must never meet, for it is written in the Ancient prophecies that a young Woman and a young girl shall be united as one to bring destruction to all those who oppose the light of this world and the worlds to come." He released the Man as he slumped down to the floor.

"Neb," the Voice spoke to him.

"Finally," the Man said.

"Neb is your name from this day forth."

Neb loved that name as the power of that name began flowing through his veins.

"You shall be called Neb because you were brought forth from the sinful nature and deceitful actions of the vessel that you possess."

Neb shook his head in agreement for he knew that, that was how he had been created.

"Who are you?" he asked, but he already knew the answer.

"Azazel," he answered.

Neb fell to his knees for that name was very powerful as well and he feared it now more than he ever did for he was speaking with the deceiver of mankind.

"I need for you to make her feel like she is not in danger. Once she relaxes, her vision will lead us to the stronger one who is much older.

"I will do as you ask," Neb said to him, obeying him.

"Good for if you allow your hunger to harm her in any way you will be punished." Just as Azazel cam he left.

Neb began walking over to the door to leave to go to the next room to check on the little girl.

CHAPTER 8

"Damn man," Sal said to Onyx approaching his Denali. "What the hell took you so long to get here?"

Onyx got out of his SUV and walked towards Sal.

"I told you that it was Sweetness b-day tonight and that I didn't want to be disturbed."

"Man fuck that shit," Sal to him angrily. "When shit is about to go down with our cheddar, its m.o.b. man. Money over bitches."

Onyx grabbed Sal by his collars and flung him against the Denali.

"Look you might call your girl a bitch, but watch your mouth about mines," he said to him angrily.

Sal shook him off.

"Damn man, I was just playing with you. I know how much you care about that girl."

Onyx released him.

"Okay so tell me what the fuck happen over here tonight that you had to call me and interrupt my night with wifey."

Sal looked around Onyx, turning his head side to side as if he was making sure that no one was watching them. Onyx watched him wondering what the hell was up with him. Sal then began telling him what had went down.

"Man, Alonzo and his wolves came out to the block around five this afternoon, talking about how shit was about to change and shit. I was like telling him that he was really beginning to play himself with all that talk about shit changing. Well I turned my back and Joey ran out the side of the house yelling and screaming that the coke had his nose on fire. I turned back around to see what was with Joey, when one of Alonzo's boys shot him in the back."

"What the fuck!" Onyx exclaimed. "Why the hell did he shoot him?"

"See man, Alonzo had got a hold of one of our shipments and had laced our shit with rat poison," Sal answered him.

"How do you know that shit?"

"Before Joey died he told me," he answered.

Onyx shook his head in disbelief.

"Man I was about to do that nigga, but something told me to fall back and let you handle this one."

Onyx shook his head in agreement.

"Yeah man," Onyx began saying. "I got this. You best believe that the nigga is a wrap."

CHAPTER 9

Maria, Sweetness' mother sat straight up in her chair and opened her eyes. She began getting goose bumps all over her body. She began rocking back and forth in her chair as her head began to hurt from the energy she was feeling.

She did not have to question what is she was feeling for she knew that it was Sweetness' energy that she was picking up on. Maria had always kept the ram's head in the middle of the altar for Oya; because she knew that she was frightened of it, and it kept her powerful force at bay. The ram's head had been a gift from Shango himself, for no mortal human could ever withstand Oya's force. She was a strong Orisha to deal with. Her face constantly changed, so you could never know when she was happy or sad or angry.

Maria was not there to help her daughter through the change and she hoped that when Oya decided to ride her, that she would able to withstand her being.

As Maria closed her eyes, memories of her spiritual initiation began to come into view in her mind. Hers was quite different, for her mother did not know what was going with her. It had skipped her mother and came more alive inside of her. It was her Grandmother who came and took her to the sacred temple in the woods. They had made her change into white clothing then they had made her lay down on a straw mat in front of the altar. She remembered that it had also been a full moon just like tonight. Maria could hear African drums beating softly in her ears as she lay there, but there was no one around playing drums. Her Grandmother had walked up to her and had given her some dark liquid to drink. As she sipped on the liquid, it burned her throat going down tasting bitter and sweet at the same time. After drinking the mixture that was given to her, she went into a deep trance. It seemed as is she was pummeling thru time as she saw black slave women surrounding her, then ancient African women began appearing to her. The drums began sounding louder in her ears, as she wanted to get up and dance with the others as they danced around her.

When she looked up into the sky, she saw what appeared to be a huge funnel cloud moving towards her. The drums began to sound as if they were beating faster in her ears. The women that were surrounding her began spinning in circles around her as if they were imitating the funnel cloud spinning towards her. Maria was not scared but nervous for the she felt safe. As the funnel cloud approached her, she could hear the women chanting OYA- OYA come, back to back. The funnel cloud approached her and stopped inches away from her feet. Maria was then lifted up to her feet by an invisible force. The force of the wind began blowing her hair down from its ponytail, and it was if the wind from the funnel cloud had transformed her hair into long beautiful dread locks. She stood their in her new countenance glowing from the energy which had begun taking her over.

All of a sudden she saw a beautiful strong woman step out of the funnel cloud wearing a mask with a multi-colored skirt on holding a horsetail whip in her hand. On her right arm she wore nine copper bracelets decorated in brown cowries. The woman stepped inside her body possessing her as she saw the spirits and souls of those who had once lived standing on a huge embankment.

She looked down and saw a river, which looked as if there were a thousand souls begging for their lives. Maria then saw a silver chalice on a rock. She used her hands to pick up the chalice and drunk all that was inside. She felt a surge of power course thru her veins and it was as if she inhaled all that was dead, and all that was about change. She then looked up into the sky as lightning began flashing, giving that which had possessed her more power. As she embraced all that was happening to her, she then saw this warrior walk towards her. He was dressed in green and black and he carried an iron machete in his hands. He walked up to her and kissed her gently on the lips while placing the machete at her feet.

"Ogun," she heard the woman say, as Ogun disappeared.

Then she saw the most beautiful man she had ever seen in her life standing right before her. He was dressed in red and white and thunder shot forth from his hands. He bent down and kissed her feet.

"Shango," she heard the woman say, as he too disappeared.

The woman then began using telepathy to communicate with her.

"My name is Oya and Yansa to some. I have come to bless you with the gift of discernment and the power to be able to communicate with the dead. Please use your gift wisely to help others. My two husbands, Oggun and Shango shall walk with you always."

Maria fell backwards on the mat as the presence of Oya left her body. Oya then picked up the machete and made 9 small cuts on her right cheek. After cutting her face, Oya disappeared.

Maria opened her eyes as she remembered how she had become the daughter of Oya knew that Sweetness would experience the same thing, but hers would be more intense. Maria was beginning to worry when she heard the voice of her Grandmother telling her that all is well and to let her mind be at peace. She then closed her eyes again and went into a deep sleep.

She began dreaming of her daughter and the powerful that change that was coming to the whole world.

CHAPTER 10

Sweetness was awakened by the sound of African drums playing in the distant. In all reality the drums were right there in front of her, but Oya had taken over her body and it felt like she was sitting in the back of a very long bus. She tried to stand but found that she had no usage of her limbs, She looked around her and realized that she was laying on a purple straw mat surrounded by nine huge cowries. Sweetness tried to scream, but no sound escaped her mouth.

"I am not going to hurt you daughter," she heard Oya whisper inside her mind.

"Who are you," Sweetness asked her silently.

"I am the beginning of change," she answered her.

"What is your name?"

"Oya."

"Where am I?"

"In the motherland."

"Africa?"

"Africa spelled with a "k" before it became the world of today."

Sweetness fears began to ease off her some as she became more aware of her surroundings. She could not believe that she was in Africa.

"How did I get here?" she asked Oya.

"I bought you here thru time," Oya answered.

"Why am I here?"

"Daughter of Oya you have been chosen to carry my energy in this world of destruction. I have chosen you and another to heal this world and make it at peace for the other worlds to come."

Sweetness shook her head in disbelief. "I got to be dreaming," she thought to herself.

"No you are not dreaming" Oya said to her softly. "You have been wearing your crown since the beginning of time. You have been chosen by the Most High to create change upon the Earth using my essence and power. In this realm and the next shall you be known."

"What do you mean by realm? "She asked her still trying to grasp the meaning of why she was where she was.

"Let me show you."

Sweetness heard what sounded like a gushing of wind in her ears, and then she felt as if her soul was spinning in a never-ending circle of her life. When the spinning stopped she was standing on the embankment of a huge river. She looked to the left of her and saw so many people of color facing her with tears in their eyes.

"Who are they?" she asked Oya.

"They are the Ancestors who await their rebirth," Oya answered.

Sweetness looked to the right and saw more people of color floating in the river.

"And who are they?"

"They are the souls who await their freedom from damnation. They want to go back to their physical form to get it right with the Most High."

Sweetness looked behind her and saw more people of color standing off in the distant rejoicing and singing songs of happiness.

"Who are they?" she asked Oya once again.

"They are the Ancestors who have gotten it right with the Most High the first time and now they rejoice in paradise."

Sweetness closed her eyes and bowed her head in humility of being showed this vision. Slowly she opened her eyes to see the most incredible thing that she could ever see in this lifetime. Before her stood an old man who looked so ancient that time seemed to have stood still in his presence. All souls that she had seen before her eyes fell to their knees giving him reference. His countenance shown so bright, that it almost blinded her eyes.

She felt Oya leave her body, and she too kneeled before the Most High. As he approached Sweetness, she felt her blood stop flowing thru her body as she saw universes being manifested right before her. When he came closer to her, she almost fainted from his power.

"What will you offer me?" the Most High asked her.

Sweetness spoke softly to him. "All that I have is myself."

He reached inside her physical form and touched her soul causing her to faint from his power.

"Do not call yourself Sweetness anymore, but the name that was given to you, Angel."

When she came to, she was back laying on her bed in the bedroom of her new house. Slowly she got up from the bed and walked into the bathroom. What she saw made her scream, for her short twists were now long silky black dread locks.

CHAPTER 11

Maria's eyes suddenly flung open as she heard her daughter cries in the spirit. It had begun, and she smiled a little at what could possibly be going thru her daughter's mind at this time. She knew that Angel was capable of handling things of the unknown better than she could ever had.

Maria began remembering how her Grandmother had taken her into those woods that night and many more nights after that. All things had to be kept a secret, for the people in her small town of Ahoskie, always wanted to label all things that were not of their god, blasphemy and witch craft.

Her Grandmother taught her a few tricks on how to help people get out of some pretty tight situations. She would sit and watch how certain people who didn't want their business to be known would creep on over to her Grandmother's house and get that secret help. Some would even go as far as to want to know what numbers to play with the local bookie. Most of her clients had been women and they were mostly concerned about whether or not their man was going to leave them. Fate could never be escaped.

When Maria turned twenty-five she moved to Raleigh to find herself a better job. In the process of looking for a job she met Mario. Mario was a Puerto Rican who had just moved to North Carolina to start his life over. They had both decided to meet that night for drinks at Apple Bee's around 8:00 pm. One thing led to another and they ended up at Mario's house having sex. Maybe it was the excitement over being away from Ahoskie without the watchful eye of her Grandmother that made her lose her virginity to him, but what ever it was, she had gotten pregnant that same night.

Mario did not want to marry her yet because he felt as if he could not provide for her financially seeing that he was starting fresh himself. Two years went by and Mario still kept insisting that the time was not right. She ended up becoming pregnant with Chance. One night she and Mario had gotten into a huge fight for Maria was ready to get married and did not want to go back home with two children and no husband. Mario had stormed out of the house and had jumped into their car. He loved his family with all his might, but he felt like he did not have enough money saved up to make it legal. He had driven to the intersection and on the intersection was a railroad track.

Mario began driving across the railroad track deep in his thoughts when all of a sudden the car that he was in, was hit by a train. He died instantly.

Maria never questioned anyone's fate, for she believed that Ogun had taken Mario with him. Reverently she prayed to Oya to help her. The President of the train company that had hit Mario's car came by her house to visit. He presented her with a check for 21 million dollars, because the lights warning you that a train was approaching had malfunction and they did not want a big lawsuit. Maria gave thanks and accepted the check. Mario had finally taken care of them thru death.

CHAPTER 12

Neb opened the doors to the room where the young girl lay sleeping. She looked so peaceful to him that he almost allowed his humanistic side to take over and let her go back home to her mother. But of course there was no way that he could have done that for Azazel would surely destroy him.

He walked into the room over to the bed she was laying on, and stared at her. The scent of her aroma began filling his nostrils and once again the lust for her blood came back to him. Neb walked over to the window and raised it. He breathed hard inhaling the scent of the city. He smelled hunger, disease, homelessness, drugs and death. All those scents were as divine to him as the young girl scent. Neb turned around and glanced at the girl once again. He then turned around and walked out the room. Neb walked down the hallway towards his own room to sit and think. He had followed all of Azazel's instructions perfectly. He could not wait for that day when he could devour all souls of the righteous.

The little girl immediately opened her eyes once she heard Neb closing the door behind him. She rolled over and sat straight up in the bed and closed her eyes. She pulled her knees towards her chest, and wrapped her arms around them. Slowly she began gently rocking back and forth. She began wishing that she was at home with her Mother and Father. She remembered hearing her Father speaking to her telling her to be in the house before the streetlights came on.

"Zoe, make her sure you are in this house before them streetlights come on," her Father had spoken to her sternly.

"Okay Daddy," she remembered yelling out to him.

Zoe had taken her bike out of the garage, and was beginning to ride down the street to the neighborhood park. She had not even been five minutes away from her home when this man had pulled up beside her on the street. The tire on the car looked as if it was going to hit her bicycle, so she had attempted to dodge being hit by his car. Just as Zoe tried to turn her bike away from the moving vehicle, she hit the curb and the bike jumped and flipped with her on it. The man got out of the car and began approaching her to see if she was okay.

Zoe's heart began racing, because she sensed that something was wrong. She got up to run, but he had snatched her up with one move of his powerful arms and carried her to his car. He opened up the trunk and dropped her inside. That was the last time she had seen her parents.

As Zoe kept rocking, she began seeing images of those girls that she had seen in that apple. They were all screaming out to her, for her to help them be set free. Zoe closed her eyes even tighter trying to push their images and voices out of her mind.

Suddenly she saw an image of a beautiful young woman with long silky dread locs standing in a mirror. She didn't know if the woman had seen her, but Zoe mouthed out the words *'help me'* to her. The woman screamed and Zoe opened her eyes for the woman had not only seen her, but heard her!

CHAPTER 13

After the shock of seeing how long her dred locs had become, Angel just stood there admiring her image. Had she been dreaming or was this reality making her think that she had been in the presence of the Most High? It had to be reality for how else could she explain the length of her locs. The more she stared at herself she began to notice some more physical changes. As she moved closer to the mirror she saw that three tribal marks had appeared on her right cheek. She looked in the palm of her hand and in the center of her palm was a purple Ankh. She glanced back up into the mirror and for a quick moment she thought that she saw a young girl sitting on a bed. She blinked her eyes again and it was the image of a little girl that she had seen. The little girl was staring back at her. The little girl mouthed the words "*help me*", as Angel screamed.

Onyx had just pulled up into the driveway right about the time all this was going on with Angel. Just as he was about to enter the house he heard her screaming and hurriedly he went in to see what was wrong. His first instinct was telling him that someone had broken into their house and was trying to do something foul to her.

"Sweetness," he yelled out to her.

"I'm in the bathroom," she answered.

Onyx walked upstairs and went into the bathroom where she was still staring at her reflection.

"What the fuck happen to you?" he asked her staring at her dread locs.

He just couldn't believe what he was seeing for her dread locs were hanging down to her waist.

"Baby I think I am going thru a change," she answered him.

"Is it all yours?" he asked touching her locks.

"Yeah, they are mine. Nothing fake her," she said to him.

"Is that why you were screaming when I came home?"

"No Onyx," she said to him. "I was staring at myself wondering how my shit got this long when I saw this image of a little girl in the mirror asking me to help her."

"See there you go with that spooky shit again," he replied.

Angel turned around and walked out of the bathroom. Onyx followed her as she walked back into the bedroom and they both sat down on the bed. Angel laid her head in his lap.

"Speak baby girl," Onyx whispered to her, as he caressed her face.

"Onyx the craziest thing happened to me while you were gone. I had dozed off, so I think, and it was like I was in Africa surrounded by these women and all I could hear was these drums. It sounded as if those drums were speaking to me, then this woman appeared out of nowhere and told me that she was a part of me. But what really made me humble myself was when it felt like I was in the presence of the Most High, and he touched me and anointed me."

"Damn baby," Onyx said to her. "That was some dream."

Angel raised her head off his lap and sat straight up.

"It wasn't a dream, that shit was real. For how can you explain my hair?"

"I can't," he answered. "But I do know that all things are possible."

Angel gave him a puzzling look.

"What do you mean?" she asked him

Onyx began explaining himself.

"I believe that you are really an Angel. Not just because of your name. I mean look how many times you have warned me about certain things about to take place in my life and it all came to past."

Angel could never explain to anyone how she knew things, but at times she just knew what was going to happen. She looked up into Onyx's eyes.

"Baby, who cut you on your face?" Onyx said to her staring at her tribal marks.

Angel reached up with her left hand and began feeling the scars.

"See that's what I am talking about Onyx. I got these in my dream. Just like I got this purple symbol of a Ankh in the center of my hand."

She turned her hand over so that Onyx could see the marking.

"Baby you weren't dreaming. Something took place to you tonight when you turned twenty-one."

"I know Onyx," Angel said shaking her head. "I need to go home and ask my Mother what the hell is going on. She has the same cuttings on her face minus the mark of the ankh."

Onyx arose up off the bed and began changing his shirt. He put on a black t-shirt.

"I will take you to pick up your truck, and then I got to handle some business."

"What kind of business?" Angel asked him sounding alarmed.

"Street shit. Alonzo took out one of my people tonight and I need to go talk to him on some real shit."

Angel began seeing the vision of him inside that abandon building sprawled out on the floor.

"Onyx please don't go back out," she pleaded. "I can go home later on this morning."

"No I need to handle this. Alonzo has been selling laced powder to people. He got to be stopped."

Angel grabbed him by his arm. Just as she touched him she saw him lying on the floor with his eyes open. She then saw a man bending over him. It looked as if the man was trying to drink his blood. When the man turned his face around she saw what looked like the image of a demon.

"Onyx something bad is going to happen if you leave this house. I just saw…."

Onyx interrupted her. "Please do not tell me that vision. This must be handled or more people will die."

"But what about your life," she cried.

"Baby I got my burner, everything will be alright."

"I do not want to lose you!" she yelled.

"Look Sweetness," Onyx said to her. "You will never lose me. Even in the event of my demise, I will always be by your side protecting you and loving you."

Angel stood up and walked over to him.

"The Most High told me that I was to be called by Angel from now on," she said softy.

"Good, because I never did like you being called Sweetness."

"Promise me that you are going to come back home to me," Angel said tearfully.

"Death can not keep me from you."

Onyx reached down picked her up and kissed her.

As Onyx's lips touched hers, Angel tasted the kiss of death.

CHAPTER 14

Onyx pulled up to the corner of Idlewild and Lane Street and parked his Denali. He glanced in his rear view mirror, as he waited for Sal to come out of the house. For the life of him he could not understand why Sal had chosen to live in the middle of the hood. They both had gotten so much dough together, that Sal could live anywhere he wanted to. It wasn't like Sal had to be out on the block doing hand to hand anymore. They had foot soldiers to do that, but Sal insisted on staying in the hood. He told Onyx that he just couldn't leave his people behind. Onyx understood that somewhat, but he still did not like the fact that all it did was make him more vulnerable to the wolves.

Onyx glanced back into his rearview mirror once again as he saw Sal walk up behind the truck. Onyx unlocked the door for Sal to get in the truck.

"Man what took you so long?" Onyx asked him.

"I was trying to get that last nut from old girl," Sal answered, licking his lips.

"You always putting your dick in something," Onyx said shaking his head from side to side.

"Man she won't leave me alone," Sal said smiling.

"Whatever man," Onyx said to him. "Show me where this Alonzo rest his head at."

"Let's go over to Bragg," Sal said to him.

Onyx put the car in drive and began driving over towards Bragg Street.

Alonzo stepped out the porch and took in some deep breaths. That fresh air was feeling good to his lungs. He blinked his eyes a little to really wake up. He kept having these black outs, and when he would come to himself, he would feel a little hazy and a little lost. He would have no memory of what happened to him during these spells. Alonzo often found himself feeling very vigorated and full of energy after these spells. He knew that he was not a good person, for he would call upon his lower energy to do the things that he did in the street. He remembered one time that he had been out drinking all night and could not find a single bitch to fuck. He was walking home from the Sports Bar, when he saw this young girl walking home. He knew that she was only a child and that she had no business walking home by herself. He approached her and asked her if she needed him to walk with her. The little girl looked at him becoming hesitant at first, but then she agreed for it was late. She knew that her mother really didn't care, so she told him that he could walk with her home. As he began walking with her, the wind had picked up, and the little girls scent began filling his nostrils. For some unknown reason, Alonzo could smell that she was a virgin. He began feeling sharp jabbing pains in his head and then he just blacked out. The next morning while he was watching the news, they began telling the story of how this little girl was found brutally raped and murdered behind some houses on Poole Road. He recognized the little girl as the one that he had started walking home that night. But he didn't remember anything else about her.

He wasn't a regular street hustler, but one who liked to use the product that he sold to hurt people. Alonzo hated the crack fiends and the heroin addicts. He didn't know who the worst of the two was, but he hated them both. Especially the bitches that would always want to put their nasty ass mouths on his dick for that rock or that smack. But

43

more than that, what he hated the most was these so-called drug dealers, especially the one on the streets known as Onyx. Alonzo hated him with a passion for when he went to him for work, Onyx treated him like he was a piece of shit in front of all his boys. Alonzo could never figure out why Onyx did him like that, until one day he heard from his man that Onyx had found out that that Alonzo had used to date Angel. Shit! They had only been in the in the ninth grade and the shit had only lasted two weeks. Nevertheless Alonzo vowed that he would get him back and that is why he had begun lacing his coke with rat poison. He had only wanted to make a few people sick at first to get them to buy somewhere else, but then that shit got good to him, and he started adding more rat poison to his shipment, until the fiends starting dying.

He had told Joey, one of Onyx's soldiers, for he knew that Joey would tell Onyx, but he was not ready for Joey to blab to Onyx so quickly. He had to kill him. Sal had seen him kill Joey and he knew that once Sal told Onyx, Onyx was on his way. Alonzo reached down into his pocket and felt his burner. He looked down the street and walked back into the house.

Onyx pulled up next to the mini-park on Bragg Street and parked his Denali. After turning off the engine he and Sal got up and began walking up towards the street. Sal spotted the house that Alonzo was in and nodded his head.

"Okay look," Onyx whispered to him, "You go around back and I will go through the front door. When you hear me say word, you know it's a wrap."

Sal nodded his head and walked around to the back of the house.

Slowly Onyx crept up on the front porch with his ratchet in his hand. He knew that Alonzo would be waiting for him, so he had to be extra careful. When he got to the front door he notice that that the door was slightly ajar. Slowly he pushed it open and went in.

"What the fuck is that smell?" he asked himself, covering his nose with his hand.

It smelled liked someone had died up in there.

He opened the door to the first room that he saw and peeked in, no Alonzo. Onyx turned around and kept walking down the hall. When he got to the second room that he saw, he kicked open the door and saw Alonzo sitting on the floor Indian style with his eyes closed.

"Get the fuck up," Onyx said to him.

Alonzo opened his eyes and looked at him.

"Nigga did you hear what I said?" Onyx asked him.

Slowly Alonzo began raising himself up off the floor.

"Stop playing and get this over with," Alonzo said to him.

"I know you strapped, so give me that shit," Onyx said referring to his burner in his pocket

."Come and get it," Alonzo said challenging him.

Onyx began walking over towards him. As he moved closer Alonzo reached in his pockets Onyx pulled the trigger and shot him in his hand.

"Bitch I didn't tell you to move," Onyx yelled at him.

Alonzo grabbed his hand in pain and felled to his knees.

Onyx moved closer and tried to grab him to snatch him back up but fell with him. As he fell with him, Alonzo sniffed him, and then he began convulsing as if he was having a seizure. Onyx backed up off of him and moved against the wall. Alonzo rose straight up in the air and floated over to Ony. Onyx shot at him three times but the bullets seem to bounce off of him.

"Where is she?" he heard Alonzo asked him in a deep voice.

"Where is who?" Onyx asked back, not showing any signs of fear.

"I smell the chosen one on you. Where is she?"

"I do not know who the fuck you are talking about", Onyx answered.

"Where is she?" he asked him again.

"Alonzo I am here to kill you, not to play these sadistic games," Onyx said getting angry.

"This ain't Alonzo bitch!"

He then picked Onyx up and flanged him against the wall. He could smell Angel all over Onyx. Her essence was so strong that it was driving him crazy and he knew that Onyx had lain with her and had even tasted her. Onyx got up of the floor and fired his gun again but the bullets still did not do any damage to Neb.

"Tell me where she is," Neb demanded, as he started moving towards Onyx.

Just as Neb approached him, Onyx thought he heard what sounded like a little girl screaming for help coming from underneath the floor. It took his attention away for a second, and that's when Neb lifted him high above his head and slammed him down on the floor.

"I can smell that bitch's scent on your breath," Neb said to him.

And then Onyx knew he was talking about, Angel.

CHAPTER 15

As Onyx lay on the floor face down gasping for what seemed like his last breath, he could hear a little girl's voice screaming for someone to help her. There was a crack in the floor, and as he peered down into the crack, he could see a little girl sitting in the middle of a bed holding an apple. She wasn't bound or anything, but he knew that she needed his help. As if she heard his thoughts, Zoe looked up into the ceiling, and Onyx could not believe his eyes. Zoe looked like a younger version of Angel!

He began remembering what Angel had said about seeing the face of a little girl staring at her in the mirror. Could this be the same little girl? Maybe he should have listen to her when she was trying to tell him about her vision. Because all he knew was that something had taken over Alonzo's body and that it wanted Angel.

Neb looked at Onyx on the floor and the scent of the CHOSEN one was driving him insane. Angel's scent was stronger than the one he had downstairs in the room in the basement. She had to be the one that Azazel had wanted. What kind of power would Azazel give him if he had both of them together? He wanted to be like him to be able to pass from one physical body to the next just by touch. But that would come later, because now he had to get Onyx to tell him where he was hiding her.

He looked down at Onyx on the floor, reached down with one hand and pulled him up to his feet.

"Are you going to tell me where she is?" Neb asked him again.

Onyx looked at him and spitted in his face.

"Fuck you," he said to him through gritted teeth.

Neb flung him through the floor and he landed beside Zoe's bed.

She let out a scream as Onyx lay there with blood coming from his mouth.

Neb jumped down through the floor and stood over Onyx.

"This bitch must have some good pussy for you to give your life for her. I'm trying to spare your life, but you want to protect her."

"I don't know what kind of demon or fucked up thing you are, but I will never tell you where Angel is!" Onyx yelled in agony.

"Mmmm, Angel," Neb said licking his teeth.

"Stay away from her," Onyx yelled at him.

Zoe looked at Neb, and with her mind flanged him across the room. She then jumped off the bed and got on the floor beside Onyx.

"I'm not strong enough by myself to fight him off. Please get up," she pleaded with Onyx.

Onyx looked up at Zoe and attempted to raise himself up of the floor. He was in so much pain he didn't know if he could get up.

All of a sudden he saw Zoe being raised up of the floor. She was placed back on the bed, and he saw what seemed like hands coming up out of the bed holding her down.

"That was not nice of you, you little bitch," Neb said walking over to the bed.

"Leave us alone!" Zoe screamed at him.

A hand then came out of the bed and covered her mouth.

Onyx finally managed to stand up and he tried to walk over to Neb to prevent him from hurting Zoe. Neb turned his head towards him and froze Onyx in his tracks.

"I'm tired of playing this game."

Neb then moved over to Onyx.

"Since you won't tell me where she is then I will eat it out of you."

Onyx tried to speak but it was as if his vocal chords had been snatched out of his throat. He tried to walk but his feet seemed to be melted into the floor. He looked over to the bed at Zoe and felt helpless. With one swift hand Neb reached over and snatched out Onyx's heart. Onyx's body dropped to the floor like a bag of bones. Neb bent down and began eating at his throat, tasting Angels' essence and satisfying his thirst for blood.

Sal had been watching from the hole in the ceiling above and ran from the house with all his might.

CHAPTER 16

Angel got in her truck after Onyx had dropped her off and began driving back to her mother's house. She hoped that her mother was awoke, because she had a lot of things that she needed to ask her. She pulled up into the driveway and parked her truck. As she got out of the truck, she saw the light was still on in her mother's room. Yeah, her mother was still up and she had a lot of questions to ask her.

Maria looked out the window when she heard Angels' truck pull up outside. Maria knew that she would have to answer all of her daughter questions.

"Ma," Angel yelled out to her, as she entered the house.

"Stop yelling before you wake Chance up," Maria said to her walking down the stairs.

When Maria looked at Angel she was taken back by her appearance. Her daughter no longer looked like her daughter, but the daughter of OYA for real. Her locs were massive flowing down past her shoulders to her waist. The tribal marks on her face were more intense than hers. More defined. As she looked up into her eyes, there seemed to be fire hidden behind her pupils. Maria did not now if it was coming from her anger or her possession.

Angel placed her keys and her purse on the couch and walked over to her mother.

"Ma please explain to me what took place with me tonight?" she asked her mom.

Maria looked at her daughter in the eyes.

"Follow me," she told her,

Angel followed her mother down stairs to the basement. She stood there watching as she saw her mother open up a door to a secret room. She then followed her mother inside the room.

"What is all this?" Angel asked her mother, looking around the room.

There were African paintings on the walls and tables set up in the room with different objects on them. In the center of the room she saw the table with nine purple candles burning with a rams' head placed in the middle of the table. To her right she could see an altar with pictures of old people hanging over the table.

"All this is your explanation," she answered her daughter.

Maria pulled out a stool from under the altar and placed it beside the altar for Oya.

"Ma, why are all those tables set up like that?" Angel asked her mother looking at the shrines that were set up for the Ancestors and the Orishas.

"I want you to listen to me and when I finish talking then you can ask all the questions you want to ask me."

Maria walked over to the Ancestors altar and sprayed it with holy water. She then walked over to her daughter and sat down beside her on the floor.

"When the slaves were brought over here from Africa, they did not know about Christianity, for they worshipped the Most High in truth and with nature. All life contained an energy or spirit and that is what they honored. We as a black people live within circles. Our circle is the Most High, surrounded by the Ancestors. Surrounding them are the Orishas, and all other spirits. This universe is mass so there are many energies that I am not familiar with, but the ones in which I am familiar with, are the ones that surround us and protect us. You see our Ancestors were the Yoruba people and they worshipped the Orishas. The slave masters of our people tried to make them forget about their past, but the Most High keeps it alive in some of us. I know that it may seem secretive, but what the world do not understand they want to label it as evil, when in fact the evil was done when they tried to strip us of our identity and culture and then call us pagans and uncivilized. See Angel the biggest altar I have is to our Ancestors. We must first and foremost honor them, and then all else will follow. The food you see placed on the altar is to feed their energy and let them know they are not forgotten. I give them libation to let them know that they are honored."

"Is that like when I see my boys pouring liquor on the ground to one of my friends who got killed?" Angel asked her.

"Yes exactly. The rest of my altars represent the major Orishas in our life. They also help us with day-to-day matters to keep balance in our life. The one that you are sitting close to is to be that of Oya. She is our guardian Orisha and it seems like you are her true daughter. See when you turned twenty-one she came here looking for you, for you have been chosen to fulfill prophesy. You were born on February 2nd that is her born day and you carry that unusual marking on your right thigh. It was she that came to you tonight and brought you through the change."

Angel stood up and faced the altar for Oya.

"Ma she is very beautiful. But I also saw more than that."

"I know for the Ancestors took you back to our home and they initiated you. That is why you see those markings on your face."

Angel turned over her hand and showed her the marking of the ankh.

Maria bowed down in front of her daughter with her face to the floor.

"Ma what is wrong?" Angel asked her looking very concerned.

"Angel you have been touched by the MOST HIGH!" she exclaimed.

Tears began streaming down Maria's face.

"You are truly the chosen one Angel," she said to her. "I honor you."

"Ma please tell me some more, for I do not yet understand everything."

Maria looked up her daughter and told her to sit back down.

"Your mother is very powerful. OYA brings about change. She represents the lightning, fire and the winds. She is also the guardian, which helps all souls cross over to the other side. Her countenance can be so strong that she is known for destroying cities with her powerful winds, but also she brings about change."

"Did she bring about the devastation to New Orleans and the Gulf Coast?"

"Man was responsible for that disaster, but the winds did not destroy those cities. Your father Orisha is Shango. He is Oya's husband and they fight in battle together. Ogun also helps Oya for he was her first husband. You were conceived in my womb, but the spirit of Oya rests upon your crown. She has blessed you with her power and the gift to be able to see the future, spirits and all opposing energies."

Just then Angel fell back in to her mother's arms.

"What's wrong Angel?" she asked her.

"It's Onyx. Something's got him and I got to help him!" she cried.

Angel could feel Onyx becoming weak and she knew that her vision was being manifested as she spoke with her mom. Maria also could feel Onyx dying.

"There is nothing that you can do to stop this, for this is part of your destiny."

"There is no Angel without Onyx!" She exclaimed.

"Angel please calm down."

"No Ma I can't. That's my baby being hurt and I can feel him. He's calling out to me with his mind and I must go to him."

Maria grabbed her daughter by the arm. "You can't leave. I must tell you everything."

"Tell me what?"

"There is another like you, a little girl who must be united with you in order for prophecy to come to past. But there is also an opposing force trying to stop this from happening. He is looking for you and you must be ready to fight him. You are not ready to face that demon yet."

"Ma what in the hell are you talking about? First you tell me that that I have been chosen, then you tell me that there is a demon out there trying to kill me?" Angel yelled at her.

"Yes Angel exactly! You posses this great power and it goes beyond all that is great in the universe. The MOST HIGH came down and touched you and left a part of himself inside of you. You must listen to me and allow Oya to come back and teach you."

Angel looked at her mother and then pulled away from her.

"That's all good mama, but first I must get to Onyx. He's dying!"

Angel raced up the stairs and ran out the front door leaving her mother standing there. She then jumped into her Explorer and left.

Maria looked at the altar for Oya as the candles went out on its own.

"He's already dead," she thought to herself.

CHAPTER 17

Angel drove around to Idlewild then made a right on Lane Street. She was trying to see if she saw Onyx's Denali parked anywhere. She then drove over by Maple Street and down through Washington Terrace. No sign of Onyx's truck anywhere. She went back up Lane Street and after not seeing Onyx's Denali decide to drive back to their home.

While driving she began to let all that her mother had told her sink in. If she was so special then why couldn't she find Onyx? It was as if she was being mentally blocked from seeing his where a bouts. Not only that, she was finding it hard to focus for her thoughts kept going back to seeing him lying him on the floor with that demon ripping out his throat. Maybe her mother was right, but why would it kill Onyx? She also began remembering the little girl that she had seen in the mirror. She had thought that maybe it was she in her younger days for the little girl had looked just like her. All this was beginning to make some kind of sense to her. She finally arrived home and pulled up in front of the house.

When she entered the house she went straight into the living room and sat down. Suddenly she heard the front door open and she ran out into the foyer.It was Onyx, and she jumped into his arms.

"Baby I thought that you were dead!" she cried.

Onyx looked her as if in a daze."Why would I be dead baby? I told you that I had to take care of some things."

"But I felt you being hurt and I drove around the hood looking for you and shit."

Onyx looked down at her and walked them both into the living room.

"I told you about riding around trying to find me. You need to stop worrying so much," he said to her kissing her on the forehead.

Angel pulled her head back, for he had kissed her on her third eye and it had sent a sharp pain through her head and down to her toes. She touched his hands and they felt so cold.

"Damn baby you freezing," she said to him leading him to the couch.

"Well help your King get warm." Onyx said smiling.

Angel placed her arms around him, and began hugging him close to her.

Something about Onyx didn't feel right, and she began to cry.

Onyx tilted her face up to his.

"Baby why are you crying?" he asked her.

"Onyx you do not feel right. What happened tonight?"

"Shit happened baby."

Just then there she heard the doorbell ring.

"Who the hell could that be?" she asked Onyx.

"I do not know baby. Don't answer the door, and maybe they will just go away."

The person at the door began screaming Angel's name at the top of his lungs.

"Yo Angel open up the damn door, it's about Onyx."

"Baby its Sal, let me open the door and see why he is yelling."

Angel went to the door and opened the door for Sal.

Sal came in the house and began hugging her. Then he started pacing around the foyer.

"Angel I got scared and ran, but I should have done something," he said frantically.

"Done what? What the fuck are you talking about?" she asked him looking bewildered.

"Man I was waiting for Onyx to say the word for me to enter the house when I heard gun shots going off. After what seemed like hours going by and still no word from Onyx, I went inside the house and then I saw this big ass hole in the floor. I could hear these screams and then when I looked down into the hole, Alonzo was kneeling over Onyx and he was eating out his throat. It looked like he was holding his heart in his right hand."

Angel looked at Sal as if he had lost his damn mind.

"Please forgive me Angel, I could have saved him but it was to late."

"What the fuck are you talking about Sal. Onyx is the living room."

Sal looked at Angel and ran into the living room.

"Onyx!" he began yelling.

Angel followed him into the living room and walked over to Onyx.

"Sal he's right here sitting on the couch," she said to him.

Sal looked over at Angel.

"Sweet there's no one there," he whispered to her.

"Onyx is sitting right here looking at you."

Sal walked over to Angel and grabbed her face. "Stop this bullshit girl! Onyx was murdered tonight he's not here!"

Angel jerked away from Sal.

"You are lying to me Sal. Onyx came home to me. Stop telling me that my man is dead!"

Sal placed his hand over the spot where Onyx was supposed to be and it felt cold as hell to him."Baby it's his ghost. I saw him die tonight."

"No, no you're lying!" she screamed. "Get the fuck out of my house! Onyx is not dead."

Sal tried to grab Angel to calm her down, but she slapped him.

Sal stepped back and then looked at Angel.

"Baby I'm sorry, but he's dead."

Sal then glanced over at the spot where he felt the coldness.

"Onyx, please forgive me." He then ran out the front door.

CHAPTER 18

After Neb devoured Onyx, and drank all his blood, he looked over to the bed where Zoe was laying and smiled. He was glad that she had not seen what he had done to Onyx. He knew that she knew that he had killed him. All he had to do was tell him where Angel was and he had refused. Oh well.

Neb rose up from the Onyx's body and looked at the hole in the ceiling. He knew that some one had seen what he had done, but he was so busy trying to taste all of Angel's essence that he did not care. All of sudden a chill ran through his body. There had been something special about Onyx, and at that moment he had regretted taking his life. He knew that Azazel would destroy him, once he knew that he had drank the blood of the one who had been chosen to protect Angel.

Neb snatched Zoe up from the bed and fled the house.

When Alonzo came to he was sitting in the middle of Pullen Park holding the hand of a little girl. He had no clue on how he had gotten there or who the little girl was that was holding his hand. The last thing that Alonzo remembered was that Onyx had shot him in the hand. He looked down at his hand, and there were no traces of a gunshot wound. It was the same hand that the little girl was holding.

"What the fuck is going on?" he asked himself, speaking out loud.

"Please take me home to my parents," Zoe said to him.

"Who the hell are you?" Alonzo asked her.

"Zoe," she answered. "I want to go home."

"Then go home," he said to her, still looking at his hand.

"The demon that lives inside of you won't let me," she cried.

"I know that I am an evil nigga, but there ain't no demon that got Alonzo," he said shaking is head.

Zoe began crying, for some reason she had gotten this newfound strength. She had not believed her eyes when she saw the demon leave Alonzo. After all she had seen she had stopped being afraid of the unknown. As Alonzo slept she had taken his hand into hers and prayed over it. As she prayed she began hearing voices speaking to her, telling her to use the power that was inside of her, and that she should no longer be afraid, for some one was coming to help her. She had looked down into her hand and she watched in amazement as Alonzo's hand began to heal. It was as if he had never been shot. She knew that the demon had killed Onyx and she wished that she had the power to bring him back to life. She had picked up on his energy, and she felt like he had been an angel.

Zoe looked at Alonzo. "What makes you think that you are evil?" she asked him.

"Man I am not about to explain shit to no little girl that I do not even know," he answered.

"You don't have to. But I see why that demon chose to live inside of you."

Alonzo looked down at her and stood up. He began feeling a soft thump-thump against his leg. He reached into his pocket and pulled out Onyx's heart.

"What the fuck is this shit!" he yelled.

Zoe gasped also, for she knew that it was Onyx's heart.

"It's his heart!" she exclaimed.

"Whose heart? What the fuck are you talking about?" Alonzo said looking down at the heart on the ground.

Zoe stood up and ran over to the heart and picked it up.

"The man that shot you in the hand," She answered, placing the heart inside her shirt. She knew that there was a reason why that heart was still beating. She felt that she had to protect it from the demon, for she knew that he was coming back.

Alonzo began pulling on his locks. If this was Onyx's heart, then Onyx must be dead.He could not remember killing Onyx, or snatching out his heart.

Zoe started backing slowly up towards the carousel. She was going to try to run before Neb came back. She knew that if she did not try to run now, she would never be able to leave once Neb came back. She kept on her eyes on Alonzo as he paced back and forth trying to make some sense out what had happen tonight and why he could not remember a damn thing. Once Alonzo's back was turned Zoe took off. She began running with all her might towards the entrance of the park. She just knew that if she made it to the entrance of the park and to the main street, that she would be rescued. Just as she approached the concession stand something grabbed her by her braids. It was Alonzo.

"Where the fuck is you going?" she heard him ask angrily.

Zoe did not have to turn around to know that Neb had returned.

CHAPTER 19

Angel fell to her knees not knowing what to do. She had seen Onyx, even hugged him, and there was no way that he could be dead. Sal had to be lying to her. Onyx got up and walked over to Angel and carried her back to the couch.

"Sal is saying that you are dead Onyx," she cried.

"Baby I think that I am," he said softly to her.

"Then how can I see you and feel you if you are dead?" she asked him through her tears.

Onyx shook his head at her. He did not know himself but he did know that he was dead.

"Angel when Sal was telling you what had happened tonight, it brought back memories of what had happened to me. All of it is true."

"No!" Angel screamed at him. "You can't be dead! You can't leave me, not now."

"Baby, I tried to fight but he was to powerful for me."

"We are supposed to get marry and live in this house together," she cried.

"Did I not tell you that death could not keep me from you?"

Angel looked up into his eyes.

"I love you so much baby," he said to her trying not to cry.

"I love you to," she said to him.

"Something happened tonight and it involves you," Onyx said to her changing the mood to a serious one.

"What do you mean?" she asked him.

"Well I was about to shoot Alonzo again when he got possessed with this demon. This thing kept asking for you, for he said that he could smell your essence all over me."

Angel stood up and walked over to the fireplace. "My mother told me some things about myself tonight. She told me that I had been chosen, and that there was this demon out there trying to destroy me."

Onyx stood up as well and walked over to her.

"It has to be the one that has taken over Alonzo," he said to her. "What else did she say?"

"She said that I was the daughter of Oya and that she was going to help me destroy this evil demon and bring peace back to our people."

Onyx looked at her. "Angel you are going to need my help as well. This fucker is strong as hell. He snatched my heart out."

Angel gasped when she heard that. How could she stand against some thing that strong?

"Baby there was also a little girl with him. And damn if she didn't look just like you."

Angel looked at him and shook her head in disbelief.

"My mother told me that there was a girl who would be joined with me in order to save our people and bring the truth back."

"Well that thing has her, and now he wants to you."

Onyx placed his arms around her and held her close.

"I promise that I am not going to let anything happen to you."

Angel pushed Onyx away from her.

"You are a fucking ghost, how can you help me?"

Onyx looked at her with hurt in her eyes. "All things are possible," he said to her.

Angel held her head down in sadness.

"Onyx I'm sorry, but who's gonna believe that you are with me?"

Onyx took her in his arms and kissed her. "What about your mother?"

Angel grabbed her keys and her purse and looked at Onyx.

"C'mon baby lets go."

CHAPTER 20

Neb grabbed Zoe's arm and went back up into the park. Zoe knew that Alonzo was never coming back, for Neb had gotten some rest and she could feel another energy force greater than his coming. Neb had taken to her to a big oak tree in the middle of the park. He felt better there sitting in the darkness of that big tree. He knew that Azazel was coming to him for he could feel his presence getting stronger. As he leaned back against the tree holding Zoe's arm, he felt a strong force pushed him back against the tree and pin him down. Zoe was pushed away from him the force as well.

"What have I done Master!" he yelled out to Azazel.

"Why did you kill her protector?" Azazel asked him.

"I could smell the CHOSEN one on him, and he would not tell me where she was," he answered.

"Did you find out anything after you killed him?"

"No," Neb answered,

"Of course you did. You found out that he was her protector, and by killing him you made him that more powerful to protect her."

"I still have Zoe," Neb said in his defense.

"Yeah but she also showed her power that she possessed as well," Azazel said releasing him from the tree. "Tell me Neb what did you do with his heart?"

"It's in my pocket," Neb said. He reached down into his pocket and there was no heart. Zoe knew that Onyx's heart was special. She used her power to keep them from knowing that she had the heart hidden in her shirt.

"I had it in my pocket," Neb exclaimed.

Azazel flanged him against the tree again and began choking him. "If it wasn't that we were running out of time, I would send you back to hell where I got you from. But I still need you," Azazel said angrily,

Azazel looked down at Zoe on the ground. She was sitting there with her eyes closed and praying. Azazel tried to penetrate her thoughts but he couldn't. Damn she was stronger than what he thought. Zoe's thought were blocking him from reading her mind. He knew that she and the CHOSEN one could never meet.

Azazel released Neb once again, and Neb fell to the ground.

"Even as I stand here and fuck with you, the CHOSEN one is about to become stronger."

Neb looked at Azazel then down at the ground. "What will you have me to do?" he asked Azazel.

Azazel knew that time was running out for he was only a servitude and one of the eight prince's would be demanding a report on what had taken place.

"Go back to the house for they soon come." Azazel said then he disappeared.

CHAPTER 21

Maria sat on the porch waiting for Angel to come. It was the day after Angel's born day and a lot had taken place in less than twenty-four hours. She did not know how much Angel would be able to take, but she knew that she had to prepare Angel for her confrontation with Neb and Azazel. She stood up as she saw Angel pull up into the driveway. She had asked Chance to go over a friends house for awhile, for she did not want Chance to know what was about to take place in the basement of their home.

Angel jumped out of the truck and ran into her mother's arms. "Onyx is dead," she cried.

"I know sweetie," she said to her comforting her.

"But Ma, I can still see him," she said to her.

"Come," Maria said to her daughter. "Let's go inside."

Angel went with her mother inside the house and they went downstairs into the basement. Maria sat Angel down on the stairs, and started lighting all the candles on the altars. As she lit the last candle on Oya's altar the rams head began to move and it fell to the floor. Angel bent down to pick up the ram's head, and her mother stopped her.

"Leave it," she said to her. "Maman's coming."

Just then a gust of wind came inside of the room and when Angel looked up towards the ceiling she saw a small whirlwind. Inside the whirlwind was Oya wearing a mask. She was holding a silver chalice, which she gave to Angel to drink from.

"Drink," Oya commanded her.

Angel took the chalice and drunk all the thick dark liquid from the cup. She began to get light headed and she felt as if she was going to faint. Maria rushed to her side and held her up. Angel handed the chalice back to Oya.

"The mixture will give her power to overcome Onyx's death for now and help her to focus," Oya said to Maria.

Angel began regaining her strength and sat straight back up to listen to what Oya had to say.

"Onyx can take her to where Neb is, but there is not too much he can do without his heart."

"I am his heart," Angel said with strength in her voice.

"Yes you are," Maria said to her.

"Please just tell me what I have to do to destroy this demon and make sure that no more will come back to hurt me nor my family," Angel said to Oya.

Oya stepped out of the whirlwind and stood beside Maria. She waved her hand at and whirlwind disappeared.

"She must take the initiation of the Palo," Oya said to Maria.

Maria began shaking her head. "No I do not want her to do that," she said back to Oya.

Oya pushed back her table and things started flying across the room.

"Do you not know that she is protected?" she asked Maria.

"Yeah I know, but is it needed?"

"To fight Neb and Azazel, she needs all."

Angel looked at both of them. "I will do whatever it takes to save my people," she said boldly.

Just as she said that three Ancestors appeared out of nowhere, including Onyx.

"Let's prepare," Oya said to them.

Maria got a white pail from behind the Ancestors altar and filled it with warm water and herbs for Angel's bath. She then told Angel to stand up as she cut her clothes off of her and began bathing her in the warm herbal bath. Once that was done she handed Angel a red robe and told her to put in it on. She then covered Angel's locs up in a red head wrap. Maria then took a piece of the red cloth and tied it around Angel's eyes. She lit a white candle and handed to her daughter to hold the candle and pray.

Angel began becoming nervous as she sat there holding the candle in her hands. After what seemed like forever she was picked up and led into another room that she did not know existed in her mother's basement. Two of the Ancestors were standing beside her and one was standing in the back of her. They escorted her through the door into the room and Angel could hear an animal moving around. It sounded like it was a rooster as she heard him making noises. Angel began praying that the MOST HIGH would allow her to skip this initiation, for she was becoming afraid. Just then she started shaking and she felt something enter her body. It was Onyx.

"I'm right here with you baby," he said to her softly.

She was given a liquid to drink and as she drunk the red hot fiery liquid, she began to swoon. She could hear African drums beating in the distance and they seemed to get closer as the liquid was taking over her body. Angel closed her eyes and fainted to the floor.

When Angel opened her eyes she heard the growl of an animal at her feet. When she looked towards her feet she saw what looked like the biggest lioness she had ever seen. As quick as she saw it, it vanished. Angel laid back on the floor and closed her eyes. The top of her head felt sore and when she placed her hand up to touch her forehead she felt small cuts over her third eye. She looked at her hands and there were small cuts on each side of her hands. She looked down at her legs and pulled her robe up. She saw that there were small cuts on her legs as well and she could feel the cuts made on her back. She tried to talk but it felt as if there was a penny lodged in her throat. Angel laid back down the floor and closed her eyes. Just as she was about to go back to sleep she felt a nudge at her side. When she opened her eyes, she saw the image of mutilated bodies standing around her. She jumped up and ran to the door to try to get out, but the door was locked. She then heard this voice tell her to listen to the message that they were bringing her. Angel walked back to the mat on the floor and sat down.

"We have come to ask you for help in crossing over to the other side," they all said in unison. "Once you defeat Neb then we can be released to be reborn back into the physical to get it right this time."

Angel nodded her head in agreement then they all disappeared. She looked over to the corner of the room and saw a huge iron pot sitting against the wall with African statues surrounding it. The statues looked as if they were all smiling at her. Just then the door opened up and Maria entered the room.

"Ma what happened to me," she asked Maria.

"You took Palo," she answered.

"But I saw these ghost with heads cut off and arms missing form their bodies," she said back to her.

"Yes you were supposed to see that," her mother said bluntly.

"What's wrong?" Angel asked her mother.

"Nothing," her mother replied. This was not the time for her to show any signs of emotions towards her daughter. "Its time for Onyx to take you to back to that house, they are waiting for you."

Angel looked past her mother and saw Onyx standing there. Onyx walked up to Angel and placed his arms around her.

"Do not worry, I'm never leaving you," Onyx said to her.

Maria held her head down when she heard him say that. She knew that Onyx would have to leave her once he got his heart back.

"I am ready," Angel said to both of them.

"Angel do you remember when you had your initiation with Oya?" Maria asked her daughter.

"Yes?" Angel answered her.

"Well they gave you gifts, use them." Maria said to her.

Angel grabbed Onyx's hand and looked at her mother.

"I have my Ogun and Shango right here."

CHAPTER 22

Zoe was back in the middle of the bed staring at the red apple again. She felt within herself that some thing was about to happen in that house. She tried to use her mind to contact Angel again, but Azazel had placed and invisible negative force of energy around her bed, and it was preventing her from using her powers.

Neb was above her patching up the hole in the floor trying to keep him self busy while waiting for The Chosen one and her protector to come. Azazel had given him more power to help him with his confrontation that he was waiting to have with her. He needed it be enough for he was unsure of what kind of power she possessed. He looked down into the room where Zoe was and smiled to himself. Soon he would have her as well.

Onyx guided Angel straight to the house where his body laid. He wished that he still had his burner, but he knew that would not help him against Neb. He had seen all that Angel was and it made him love her more. They say that love conquers all, but tonight he needed Angel to hate with all her might, for that was what was needed to kill that demon and send it back to hell.

Neb stopped what he was doing. He could feel the Chosen ones energy and it was driving him crazy. Her scent was so righteous that he knew that he would never get enough of drinking her blood. No he would not penetrate her for she was not a virgin, but he would drink her blood nevertheless. He walked into the next room and looked at Onyx's body lying there on the floor.

"What the fuck did I do with is heart?" he asked himself.

Just then he heard door open and he went downstairs to wait for them to find him.

CHAPTER 23

Angel slowly entered the house and covered up her nose.

"Yeah I know," Onyx said to her. "The scent is to die for you."

"You got jokes huh," Angel said to him chuckling.

"Just trying to make you feel at ease," he said to back to her.

Angel began feeling a negative energy coming from downstairs. She told Onyx that they needed to go downstairs, for that was where Neb was.

Onyx felt that energy as well as followed her down the stairs. Angel opened the door to the basement room and went in. There sitting on the bed was the little girl whom she had seen in the mirror. Zoe was sitting in the middle of the bed looking at her. Angel walked over to the bed and tried to reach her but something was blocking her from getting near her on the bed.

"He has some kind of shield around me," Zoe said to her.

Angel waved her hand as lightning began to come out of her hands, causing the negative energy to vanquish from around the bed and she was able to get to her. Zoe fell into Angel's arms as they both hugged each other tightly.

"Well, well, well, what do we have here," she heard Neb's voice say. Angel turned around and she saw a young man about Onyx height standing before her. He was very muscular and his locks looked like tiny snakes dangling from his head. His eyes were a dark orange and, and there was blood coming from his mouth.

"What do you think," Angel answered not showing any signs of fear.

"We have been waiting for you," he said to her.

"Well sorry it took so long, but I was busy getting power and shit," she replied smirking.

"Well that shit is not going to help you here." Neb then used his power to separate her from Zoe.

"No!" Zoe screamed as she fell back on the bed.

Angel looked at Neb and laughed. "Is that all you got?" she asked him.

"Bitch you're going to wish that it was!" he snarled at her.

As he tried to run up on her, Angel closed her eyes and floated across the room to the door. Onyx stood there looking at her in awe. He could not believe that she just did that. Neb turned around and Angel then thrust her hands forward and balls of lightning with fire shot forth knocking him to his knees.

"I see Shango has blessed you well," Neb said as he got up from the floor.

Neb closed as his eyes as fire began raining down top of Angel's head. Angel began chanting causing rain to come forth putting out the fire. Neb then raised his hands in the air causing huge hairy like creatures to come out the walls to attack her. Angel pulled out the machete of Ogun and began killing them.

As Onyx stood there looking at them battle he felt weak all of sudden. This was the place where he had died and the negative energy was killing him for he did not have his heart.

"Help me," Angel said to him through gritted teeth.

"I'm getting weak for I need my heart," he said weakly.

"You mean this," Zoe said as she took out his heart and placed it high in her hands above her head.

"Yes," Angel and Onyx said in unison. Angel then used her lightning and took the heart from Zoe and gave it to Onyx.

"No," Neb yelled as he saw Onyx take his heart and place it upon his chest.

Neb rushed over to Onyx, just as he was about to grab Onyx around his throat, they all heard a gun shot. Neb dropped to his knees as Sal rushed in with his 9mm and began rapid firing at Neb.

"Die mother fucker!" he screamed. "Die!"

The bullets went through Neb and as he rose up from his feet, he looked at Sal and yelled. Sal's body split into three pieces as his head rolled over to Onyx's feet.

Onyx looked down at his boys' head and opened his mouth. Fire came from his mouth and went directly to Neb. Those tiny snakes dangling from his head were consumed instantly. Neb's eyes went from dark orange to black as he tried to make a dash towards Zoe. He knew that he was defeated, but he would not allow Zoe and Angel to unite.

Angel realized what he was doing and she jumped on the bed to where Zoe was. Angel yelled out the name Oya, and as she did, a mighty wind came through and Zoe and Angel merged as one. As they did the roof of the house opened up and a tornado came down and sucked Neb up taking him back to hell.

Angel fell back on the bed as Onyx ran by her side.

"Angel," Onyx said to her. "Are you all right?"

Angel began coming to her self as she felt Onyx holding her close.

"Yes baby," she answered him.

"Where's Zoe?" he asked her.

"She's part of me now. We have to be as one until my people are brought back to their proper place," she answered Onyx.

They both glanced over to the remains of Sal's body lying on the floor. Angel looked towards the door and saw Sal standing there.

"Man I went out like soldier," he said to Onyx.

"Yeah right man that was a dummy move."

"True that," Sal said to him. "But it is what is, and I had to do what I had to."

Onyx smiled at him. "You just couldn't live without me faggot," he said to him smiling.

"True that. But now I must say good-bye for my chariot waits. Who knows, maybe I will come back as a boss this time."

They looked up in the sky and saw a chariot descending down into to the room to pick Sal up. Just as Sal was about to get on the chariot, the apple that was lying on the bed beside Zoe exploded, and the trap souls of the girls that Neb had molested were released also as they ascended up in the sky with him as well.

CHAPTER 24

Angel and Onyx drove back over to her mother's house and pulled up into the driveway, Angel turned off the car and looked at Onyx.

"What's wrong bay?" he asked her.

"I feel like your work is done here with me," she said to him.

"Naw, baby," he said shaking his head in disagreement. "I ain't ever leaving you."

Angel opened the door and they both went into the house. Maria was sitting on the couch waiting for them to come into the house. Her daughter had done a good job destroying Neb by using all of her positive energy to overcome his negativity. She knew that from this experience Angel also used her power to call upon Oya, and Yansa had come with all her might. Had it been Oya or had it been Centella Ndoki who had came in the tornado and carried Neb away?

Angel walked over to Maria and gave her hug. "I knew that you could do it," she said to her daughter.

"Ma it wasn't me, but the power Of the MOST HIGH helping me with his divine Orishas," she answered back.

"That is exactly what I wanted to hear," Maria said smiling.

She pushed her daughter away from her and looked down into her face.

"You are not the same as you were yesterday," she said to her.

Angel took her mother hands and raised them to her lips and kissed them.

"I'm not the same as I was an hour ago," she said back to her. Angel looked at her mother and spoke. "You know I feel Zoe inside of me."

"She is a part of you now," her mother responded sadly.

"What about her parents? Do we not have the responsibility of letting them know what has happened to their daughter?"

"Angel her parents were her guardians of this realm. They already knew that she would never return back to them. They were prepared for this day, and believe you me, they know that her energy is safe and is with you. All they have to do is call out to her and she will go to them in her dreams."

Maria stood up and pulled Angel up with her. "Come," she said to her as she led her back downstairs into the basement.

"Why we going down there?" she asked her following her.

"You got to help Onyx cross over."

Angel stopped walking. "No he can't leave me," she said.

"Angel, Onyx was a good man. Even though he did those things in the streets, his heart was still pure at the end. He must go to a place of resting."

"But what about his body, doesn't that have to be buried back into the Earth from which it came from?"

"No baby we don't follow those laws. His body has no bearing anymore. He has his heart back and he needs to cross over."

Angel went with her mother into the room, and on the floor she saw some of Onyx's personal belongings on a white piece of fabric. There was a coconut, a bowl of water, and a bottle of rum placed on the cloth as well.

"You already got his stuff from my room," Angel said to her mother softly.

"He has to be gone by the third day," she answered her.

Her mother lit a candle and placed it in the cloth beside the coconut. She then began praying as she saw Onyx materialized before her eyes.

Onyx grabbed Angel's hands and kissed them.

"Please don't leave me baby," she cried.

"I will always be here with you," Onyx said through is own tears.

"I wish you hadn't gotten your heart back, she cried.

"You are my heart," he said to her.

Onyx looked at Maria then back at Angel.

"When you go home tonight look in the top drawer I got a surprise for you."

Angel stepped back from Onyx as he held her in his arms and kissed her.

"I love you Angel Jones," he said to her.

Maria looked down at the altar for Onyx and began chanting in Yoruba his rights of passage into the next realm.

As Angel held his hands they began to fade until he was gone.

CHAPTER 25

When Angel left he mother's house and got home, she felt so empty and lonely inside. This house was supposed to be for her and Onyx. She vowed to herself that she would never be with another man as long as she lived.

She went inside and went upstairs to their bedroom. She took off her clothes and showered. She slipped on her purple gown then climbed into the bed. As she lay there she looked up into the ceiling and she saw her mother Oya floating above her.

"Greetings Maman," she said to her as he bowed her head in honor.

"Angel I have come to tell you the fight is not over. As long as Azazel still has power over this Earth, he will continue to send his demons out to destroy you and Zoe."

Angel looked at Oya and closed her eyes.

"I know Maman, and with all that I posses inside of me, including Zoe will fight until the end."

"You have the power of three inside you and never be afraid to use that power. It doesn't even matter what man thinks of you for the MOST HIGH has chosen you."

Angel bowed her head in honor again, and Oya was gone. Angel got up from the bed and went to the drawer that Onyx had told her to go. She opened the drawer and it was filled with nothing but hundred dollar bills. On top of the money was a note.

Dear Angel,
  This dough right here should help you with your college education and whatever you want to do with your life. When you were passed out after receiving Palo, I had your mother help me with this. In the bottom drawer you will find my will leaving everything that I own to you. And I do mean everything. I love you girl.
  Always Onyx

Angel reached into his second drawer and pulled out a white tee shirt. She slipped it on. As she lay there, all of a sudden she felt his side of the bed sink in. She then felt Onyx's arms engulfing her in a warm embrace. Angel closed her eyes and smiled.

"Not even death can keep me from you," Onyx said as they both fell fast to sleep.

Made in the USA
Middletown, DE
06 November 2023

41908549R00051